WORDS FROM THE CROSS

WORDS FROM THE CROSS

Stephen C. Rowan

TWENTY-THIRD PUBLICATIONS
Mystic, Connecticut

Twenty-Third Publications
P.O. Box 180
Mystic, CT 06355
(203) 536-2611

ISBN: 0-89622-354-x
Library of Congress Catalog Card Number 87-51281

Edited by John G. van Bemmel
Designed by William Baker
Cover design by Kathy Michalove

*All illustrations in this book,
including the cover,
are by Pauline McGrath, O.P.*

CONTENTS

WORDS FROM THE CROSS

INTRODUCTION

Reflections on the seven "words" that Jesus spoke from the cross are traditionally part of the *Tre Ore* service for Good Friday. That service, which is distinct from the liturgy for the day and consists of prayers, sermons, and reflective music, encourages an identification with the mind of Christ by focusing on his words from the cross as recorded by the evangelists.

In writing these reflections, I have kept in mind an audience that is both intelligent and faithful. People who read this book are well aware of what counts as knowledge and the way to "success" in our society. At the same time, these people also know that something is missing from society's account of the "good life." They are waiting for a truly effective and enriching word (and not another cliché) that will clarify the silent mystery that surrounds us, calls us forward, and upholds us. These words of Jesus—and the cross itself—serve as touchstones of the Gospel, and for that reason they are offered to us as the words we need to hear and are waiting for.

In reflecting on Jesus' words, I have relied on the work of contemporary biblical scholars who have taught us how to read the Scriptures better, especially by putting each word of the Gospels into the context of the kind of work the Gospel is and into the context, also, of the Jewish Scriptures to which the Gospel writers themselves make reference.

I have drawn on the work of two contemporary theologians: on Karl Rahner for his reflections on how the Gospel words—like the truly poetic words they are—make the silent mystery present in an irreplaceable way, touch the heart of our deepest human concerns, and bring us together as a people united in our hearing of these words. From David Tracy I have learned how the Gospels as "classics" throw light on our contemporary experience and show something of the depths implied in it. They manifest what is so for us and, at the same time, they proclaim the relative inadequacy of our culture's assumptions. The Gospels—like the cross itself—offer us a sign of contradiction and a means of grace.

Finally, through René Girard's work on the scapegoat ritual, I have seen in a more radical way how the cross requires that we re-interpret history from the point of view of the victim. The judgment against Jesus is nailed to the cross, and it is from the cross that Jesus reverses that judgment. Thanks to Girard's analysis, I have caught more fire from the paradox of St. Paul: through the cross it is clear that the foolishness of God is wiser than human wisdom, and the weakness of God is stronger than human strength.

I hope that you, the reader of these reflections, will be encouraged to look for ways in which the wisdom of the cross addresses you. Although this book can easily be read in one sitting, perhaps you would prefer to take one word at a time, letting the word and the reflection on it prod the direction of your own thoughts for a couple of days before returning to the following one. Since each word is better appreciated in its context, you might want to read first the passage in the Gospel from which the word is taken. For that purpose, the passage is designated at the start of each reflection.

Father
forgive them

FIRST WORD

"Father, forgive them."
Luke 23:32-34

The Gospel writers do not describe in detail the cruelty of crucifixion. They do not say it was a punishment reserved for slaves and foreign peoples—a punishment so barbarous, in fact, that Roman law forbade crucifixion for Roman citizens as unbefitting their dignity. The Gospel writers do not mention these things because they could rely on the fact that their audience would know the painful details at first hand. For example, during the lifetime of Jesus, an insurrection of Jewish patriots was put down by Roman force and 2,000 zealots, as they were called, were crucified along the road from Jerusalem to Bethlehem as punishment for their crime. The Gospel writers do not describe the details, then; they only have to say, "He was crucified," and that is enough. The pain is obvious; so, too, is the disgrace.

Jesus is not only put to death by a punishment reserved for slaves; he is also crucified between two robbers. He is thrown in with outlaws, crucified outside the city—driven away into the wilderness like the scapegoat of the ancient ritual—so that the people might be well rid of the so-called pollution of his crime. To use a term we have invented in our time, the authorities want to make Jesus a non-person, someone with no history and no voice, with no effect on others that would detract from the power of the State, a blank where a name used to be.

Even the most arbitrary authorities, however, usually end up feeling drawn to give some explanation of their actions. But the explanation that Pilate gives is no explanation at all. Rather, it is an insult. "Jesus of Nazareth—King of the Jews," he writes. And when the Jewish leaders protest that Pilate should have written that Jesus only "claimed" to be a king, Pilate replies with lordly Roman contempt for a subject people, "What I have written, I have written."

Christian belief recognizes in Pilate's inscription the truth that Jesus is, indeed, a King. But Pilate did not intend a tribute to Jesus, but only contempt for Jesus and his people. This outlaw, he says, this non-person, this slave of Roman law is your king.

And the crowd around the cross has no less contempt than Pilate does. Taking their cue from the violence sanctioned by public authority, the crowd turns on Jesus with mockery for all of his past claims to be the Messiah. It is as if they want some reason not to believe in the hope he had offered them. He had claimed and had tried to show them that in his person the Kingdom of God had come. This is too much for them to accept, and so they throw back at Jesus the words and deeds of hope he had offered. "He saved others," they say; "let him save himself." "He trusts in God; let God deliver him now. . .for he said, 'I am the Son of God.'" "Let the Christ, the King of Israel, come down from the cross—give us one more miracle—that we may see and believe." They turn all the loving deeds and hopeful words of his ministry to laughter and contempt.

And as if contempt and mockery were not enough, the disgrace of this death can be heard also in the sounds of soldiers casually throwing dice, gambling for what little remains of the prisoner's possessions, indifferent to the entire affair— only doing their job. . . only following orders. . . all in a day's work.

The Gospel writers do not dwell on these details of the crucifixion: the pain, the contempt, the mockery, the indifference. They mention these, but each writer in his own way tries to draw our attention to what the details mean.

In the words of St. Luke, from whom we take the first words of Jesus from the cross, the crucifixion is the "hour" of the power of darkness. That is, on the cross we see fully revealed the mystery of evil as it is let loose on the innocent: full of hatred, with the intent to kill.

Most of us, I think, have been taught to see the death of Jesus as all for the best, and in a certain sense this is true. But all too often this idea encourages us to take the death of Jesus for granted. We forget the full horror of it; we lose sight of its full message. The cross shows the twisted work of the power of darkness: the mystery of evil let loose on the innocent, full of hatred, with the intent to kill.

For the secular and religious authorities of the day, the death of Jesus is intended to be a political convenience—a final solution—a way out of a political and religious embarrassment. In fact, the death of Jesus, according to Luke, is the result of a deal between Pilate and Herod, a way of keeping the peace between wary politicians. With Jesus out of the way, they think life can return to normal; there will be no one to ask questions, in the name of God, about public and religious policy.

This is the horror of the cross: its brutal and effective attack on the innocent in the name of the highest authorities of secular and religious life. And we need to recognize this horror; what is more, we need to recognize how we ourselves share in this horror before we can truly understand the first word of Jesus from the cross.

We share in this horror every time we sin. And I do not use the word "sin" loosely. By sin I mean doing deliberate harm to the innocent; striking out at God through the neighbor or even through the ways in which we can misuse ourselves. Sin means inflicting pain, contempt, and mockery on what deserves respect; it means treating with indifference what should receive our attention and service.

If anyone thinks that sin is only a word that preachers use, that person should have to endure hearing a child's confession. Because children are so sensitive to the hurting power of evil, and as much as they may be aware of the things they have done wrong or should have done better, they will tell you, without really intending to, about what they have suffered. They may have neglected their chores or shown their anger or teased their siblings, but when you ask them why, you will often find a story of parents who do not like them very much, who do not care for them, who are not there for them, who do not talk to them, who strike out in anger against them—who do everything but put the child away.

Sin attacks God above all through the innocent, and not only through children. Jesus is on the cross because of all kinds of sin, and it is sin disguised, too, as enlightened self-interest, sin that is proud of its power. Jesus is a convenient scapegoat for problems that people do not have the courage or the imagination to face in any other way. That is the full horror of the cross: how well it shows the power of darkness to shout down the word of God.

And yet the word has not died out. People still take up

the scriptures or hear the Gospel proclaimed. They still look to the cross as a focus for their faith. And from the cross comes a reason for hope: the first word according to St. Luke: "Father, forgive them; they do not know what they are doing."

In fact, according to the Greek verb he uses, Luke tells us that Jesus kept saying these words over and over. And with these words, Jesus overturns what the world thinks of itself; he reverses the verdict against him; he shows that the intended scapegoat is innocent. With these words, Jesus convicts the world of sin: "Father, *forgive* them." They may have used the appearance of a trial for him, but they are the guilty ones. They may think they have solved the problem of political inconvenience, but "Father...they do not know what they are doing."

The words of Jesus completely reverse the judgment of the world. We may call him a troublemaker, an idealist, a visionary, but he keeps praying, "Father, forgive them." We think that mockery and contempt—softened, perhaps, into a fashionable cynicism—can silence the words from the cross. But Jesus keeps saying, "Father, forgive them; they do not know what they are doing."

Jesus convicts the world of sin when he prays that we be forgiven, and, at the same time, through forgiveness he breaks the cycle of endless and senseless violence and opens for us a new future. The open arms on the cross are an outstretched offer to accept the mind and the heart of Christ.

Through the words of forgiveness, Jesus makes clear what pride and the power of darkness have done. At the same time, these words make possible a time for conversion: away from sin and toward a life of innocence, toward a life lived for God in union with Christ.

The mystery of God's love is usually silent, found only

between the lines, so to speak, of our everyday lives. But in this first word from the cross, the silent mystery is present, full of grace and truth. We need to hear this word because none of us is innocent; all of us have done some harm and have tried to find an acceptable way of excusing it. To all of us, the good news comes from the cross in the first words of Jesus: "Father, forgive them; they do not know what they are doing."

Today you will be with me in Paradise

"Today you will be with me in Paradise."

Luke 23:35-43

For St. Luke, Jesus is the giver of great pardons; he is the benefactor of God's love and forgiveness. Only in Luke's Gospel do we hear Jesus say to the tax collector Zacchaeus, "Salvation has come to this house, for this man, too, is a son of Abraham." Only in Luke do we hear the parable of the good Samaritan and of the prodigal, forgiving Father. Only in Luke does the penitent woman wash the feet of Jesus with her tears and hear from him the good news, "Your faith has been your salvation; go in peace."

Because Luke wants us to know of the lavish love of Christ, he records as the first words of Jesus from the cross, "Father, forgive them." Jesus dies, then, as he has lived: full of grace to the end. Not only is the love lavish, but, according to Luke, the pardon and peace are for all, especially for those who are most at the margin of society, the people who have been written off as of no account. In this Gospel, there is no corner of the world so dark that the light of the world does not shine upon it.

In the second word from the cross, we learn that the pardon is for all, but that it can be received in different ways. Luke, it seems, wants to emphasize this. After all, Mark does not mention at all that the robbers crucified with Jesus joined the crowd in mocking him. Matthew says that *both* robbers mocked Jesus. Only Luke distinguishes between one robber and the other. The first robber joined with the crowd and said, "Are you not the Christ? Save yourself and us as well."

This is a clear cry of scorn from someone who has learned nothing from his closeness to Christ. The first robber is made only more bitter by his suffering; he has no definition of what life is for, except the life that he has left behind. And so he wants to be taken down and to be given the chance to live that life again. He is like those morally blind people in the parables of Jesus: the Pharisee, for example, or the rich man, people who are so proud and self-assured of where they stand; people who have had it their own way for so long that they cannot imagine how unreal their lives have become and how unsure their footing is. Then something happens to make them slip; in the case of the robber, he is finally arrested, put on trial, and made to account for all he has done.

Like some petty dictator deprived of his long-standing power, this robber looks only for a chance to get back what he has lost. He is shocked at the turn of events, surprised to find that fortune is fickle, and with no greater hope than what the world has already offered him, he whines to be taken down from the cross. And he mocks any Messiah who cannot give him the only kind of life that he imagines is worth living. "Are you not the Christ?" he sneers. "Save yourself and us as well."

Then the other robber speaks up, first with a rebuke to the first man and then with a clear-sighted, unvarnished admission of his own guilt. "Have you no fear of God at all?" he asks. "We got the same sentence as he did, but in our case we deserved it: we are paying for what we did. But this man has done nothing wrong."

The second thief is like the Publican of the parable or like poor Lazarus. He has no illusions about where he stands. He humbly takes stock of himself and admits that he is empty of any reason for hope that he can create for himself. In the past, he depended for his livelihood on his wits, his strength, his friends, and all have abandoned him now. He sees a certain justice in this; after all, he took his chances and lost. But what has worked its way into his imagination is the innocence and the goodness of Jesus. "This man has done nothing wrong," he says, and yet he suffers, and yet he forgives. The thief sees in Christ another way to live. He finds reason for hope in the very character of Jesus. There is some still center of peace; there is some motive for joy in the person of Jesus. And the thief, who has spent his life detecting where treasure can be found, finds it out here. He wants to share whatever goods Jesus can distribute. And so he makes his famous request: "Jesus," he prays, "remember me when you come into your kingdom."

This is the cry of every humble human heart. It echoes our most fundamental human need: "Jesus, remember me. Let me know that I matter; give me a chance to begin a new life; help me to find that total well-being we call salvation." Remember me! I have no reason for hope that I can create for myself, but I will not despair. Rather, I will count on the reason for hope that you have proclaimed through your life and brought you to the cross. "Jesus, remember me when you come into your kingdom."

The first robber had asked to be taken down; the second robber asks to be taken up: what a difference in attitude!

And Jesus, as poor as he is in everything else, is nevertheless rich in mercy. And so he answers the thief and every humble heart with the words, "Indeed, I promise you, today you will be with me in paradise." The one who humbles himself is exalted.

No doubt the authorities had intended to disgrace Jesus by crucifying him between two robbers. So much for the short-sighted cynicism of worldly wisdom! Obviously, the authorities did not know what they were doing. Jesus, we know, had eaten with sinners all of his life. He had done so in order to offer them the pardon and the peace of his company. He wanted to offer all people—even at the margins of society—a welcome into the rule of God. The company of thieves was no disgrace to Jesus; no, it was only another opportunity. After all, the Son of Man had come to seek and to save what was lost.

Summing up the life of Jesus, St. Paul reminded the Corinthians that "God was in Christ, reconciling the world to himself." And, according to Luke, even on the cross Jesus continues his ministry of pardon and peace. At the same time, the story of the second thief shows us that no one need despair of finding that mercy.

There is a reason to hope that we matter, to hope that forgiveness and life can be ours beyond any sin or death we can suffer. The thief saw that this was possible, and so he said, "Jesus, remember me. . . ." And Jesus, hearing the cry of the human heart for hope, answered him, "I promise you, this day you will be with me in paradise."

Woman, behold your son

"Woman, behold your son!"

John 19:16-27

Before the feast of Passover," according to John, "Jesus realized that the hour had come for him to pass from this world to the Father. He had always loved those who were his own in this world, and he would show his love for them to the end." In this third word from the cross, Jesus shows his love in the care he takes for the mother and the disciple.

On one level of meaning, of course, this word is spoken to Mary, the mother of Jesus, and to John, the beloved disciple. It shows the tender concern of Jesus both for the widow and the orphan. He does not want either of them to be homeless, and so he provides a home for them with each other.

But we have to remember that this word is recorded in the Gospel of John where we often find a second and even deeper level of meaning beyond the literal sense. The second meaning flows from the first, and it is suggested by the fact that Jesus speaks not to Mary or to his mother but to the woman. He uses a more formal word—almost a title, in fact—that calls to mind the first woman who was the mother of all the living and reminds us, too, of the church, the mother of all the beloved disciples of Jesus.

On this second level of meaning, Jesus shows his concern that the church should not be a widow and that humanity should not be left orphans. Rather, we are told in clear terms that we will find our home with one another. The word Jesus uses has a particularly forceful meaning in this Gospel.

We translate it as "behold" or "here," but a more accurate meaning would be *Look!*—with an exclamation point. Look and see the person I am pointing out to you. And then, look again and see the mission which that person has on your behalf. "Woman, look! *This* is your son. Son, look! *This* is your mother."

The church is the mother of humanity because, like Mary, she stands by the cross; she plants herself firmly by the side of Christ; she learns the mystery of the cross by sharing the sufferings of the cross and then she tells the story of the cross in every age to anyone who will listen. The mystery of the cross is a mystery indeed. One way I would put it is that from the cross we learn that life includes death and is stronger than death. There is no reason that this should have to be; it only *is*. "No pain, no gain" is one way to express the mystery in everyday terms; "no cross, no crown" is another. "Those who lose their lives will find them" is yet another way of saying that every share of life we receive is bought at the cost of some death. And, at the same time, every death we suffer prepares us for another way of life.

I remember talking to a couple who were suffering painfully because all they could do was wait while their young son died of cancer. They were being brave about it, and they had strong sources of support from prayer, from friends, and from their church. But still they suffered. As we talked one day, I found out what was perhaps the most difficult mystery of all for them. "Father," they said, "it isn't natural; the child should not have to die before the parents. It isn't natural. If it were us who had to go, we'd understand; we'd accept it somehow. But not our son."

It seems that death, which makes no sense in itself, makes even less sense when it comes out of place in a sequence that we imagine is reliable. I shared their anger and frustration; I had no answers to give them. All I could think to say came suddenly to mind: "But you are standing where Mary stood," I said, "at the foot of the cross. And I don't suppose that it seemed any more natural to her than it seems to you that her son had to die. I don't know why a child has to die before the parents; I don't know why anyone has to die at all. But I do believe that death is a part of life, and that God who gives us life does not give it without a purpose. Your son and you, too, can find life even through this death—or so Jesus taught us."

The church, like Mary, stands by the cross in order to witness to the mystery. And people of every age become beloved disciples precisely to the extent that they respond with faith to the news that the church has to tell. In the words of John, the mystery is this: the lifting up of Jesus on the cross is at the same time and for that very reason a lifting up of Jesus into glory. There is strange mystery here and baffling paradox, but it is a saving truth. Jesus is not only crucified but is lifted up, and when the church witnesses to this, Jesus is able to draw all people to himself.

"The church exists to serve only one purpose," says Pope John Paul II, "that each person—in every age—may be able to find Christ; that Christ may walk with each person along the path of life, with the power of the truth that is contained in the mystery of his life and saving death and with the power of the love that is radiated by that truth."

And when Paul told the Corinthians that "God was in Christ, reconciling the world to himself," he added, "and God has entrusted to us (that is, to the church) the ministry of reconciliation." From the cross, Jesus entrusts humanity to the church: "Woman, look! Here is your son and daughter." And, at the same time, Jesus commends humanity to the church: "Son and daughter, look! Here is your mother."

As his parting gift to those who were his own and whom he loved even to the end, Jesus gives the church. I know that to some people it may seem strange to think of the church as a gift. For them, the church is just a weak and sometimes even scandalous institution. Some people have met the church in the person of priests who have discouraged and angered them, youth ministers who have let them down, deacons or pastoral assistants who have disappointed them. The church in certain of her members can be a very sorry lot, indeed. Nevertheless, it is from the church that each person in the human family hears the story that makes sense of his or her own story. Each of us hears from the church the news that God's love is faithful, and that our humanity must be of great worth because it belongs to God and is wooed by God. Each of us is united to one another, and we are united to beloved disciples of all nations and all ages because each of us is hearing this word proclaimed by the church. And each of us recognizes in it something that rings true to our human experience.

Each is united to all in response to the word that comes from the church who stands by the cross and mediates the mystery.

"Woman, look! Here is your son and daughter!"

"Son and daughter, look! Here is your mother!"

FOURTH WORD

"My God, my God, why have you forsaken me?"

Matthew 27:45-47
Mark 15:33-36

W hatever it means to be human, Jesus knows it and knows it to the depths on the cross. He did not know what it is to sin, of course, but in fact it is not really necessary to know sin in order to be human. When you think about it, you realize that we were made for innocence and that sin only dilutes our humanity. It is precisely because he did not know sin that Jesus truly knows what it means to be human.

And because Jesus is human to the full, we know that he understands everything that is truly human about us, including our fears, our weaknesses, our temptations, our loneliness, our many moral dilemmas, our need for God and for one another.

In this fourth of the seven words, Jesus cries out with an

agony that every person at some time has had to suffer. "My God, my God, why have you forsaken me?" It is the most painful cry we hear from the cross; it is the most painful cry that a servant of God can make. According to Mark and Matthew who record this word, a great darkness came over the land from the sixth hour—noon—until the ninth hour.

According to Mark, Jesus had hung on the cross until the sixth hour, enduring the mockery of the crowds, the abandonment of his disciples, and even the taunts of those crucified with him. It is one hellish scene of rejection with ridicule. Jesus is so much alone. And then, at the sixth hour, even the heavens darken, and the gloom is complete. No wonder, then, that at the ninth hour Jesus cries out, "My God, my God, why have you forsaken me?"

It is no wonder that Jesus should feel—humanly speaking—this sense of desertion and even betrayal. He has spent a lifetime emptying himself for others, proclaiming God's Kingdom, even at times achieving some success at gathering disciples and inspiring the crowd. Jesus has gone about doing good, and even on the cross he has emptied himself through care for the church and through forgiveness of all. And what has come of his work? At some point, the horrible idea suggests itself that it has come to nothing. The energy of life has been spent in a blaze of activity, and all that remains are the ashes.

It is only human, then, to wonder what the Father could possibly have had in mind. What kind of life was this supposed to be anyway? At this moment, Jesus, who is fully human as well as divine, understands the suffering of all of us who do not know, at times, what has become of us or where we are going.

In the crucified Christ we have someone who understands how it feels to face a blank wall or to imagine himself trapped in a box or a cage. He knows that at those times you think that you are all alone and everyone else—including God—is getting along well enough without you. Jesus knows the washed-out feeling; the fear of never being able to get back to life; the horrible doubt that somewhere along the road of life you took a wrong turn and are too lost, now, for anything to matter. Jesus knows the isolated feeling of men and women who are divorced; of people who have deadened themselves with alcohol and drugs; of women who have been battered or even raped; of men who have been let go from work or who did not make the cut; of people who suffer bouts of depression and chronic physical disability.

In whatever way you have come to a moment of despair, you have arrived at a place that Jesus also came to know all too well. "My God, my God," he cries out, "*why* have you forsaken me?" And you will notice that the cry from the cross is not one that doubts God's existence. No, worse than that, it doubts God's wisdom. "Why have *you* abandoned me? This is not what I expected. This is not like you. This is hell."

Only if we understand this cry of anguish for what it truly is, as a real cry and as our cry, only then can we be prepared to trust that Jesus has found his way beyond our own greatest fears. The way he finds looks simple, but anyone who has tried it knows how difficult it is to take it. The way lies through trust. At the very point where Jesus is most empty, humanly speaking, of what he can do for himself, he has only two choices: either to stay in the hell of fear that God has abandoned him or to trust in God for what is coming next, despite his fears. The choice is between seeing the cross as a dead end or as a break-through.

We know that Jesus chose the way of trust because the very words he uses to express his fear of abandonment are the same words that begin Psalm 22. And although that psalm begins with real anguish, it ends with real trust that the God who is so silent now will not forget that we are made for real life, and that he will be with us to make sure that we find it.

Of course, the choice to trust is not easy. We know this from our own experience but also from a story about a man named Ivan Ilyich, told by the Russian novelist Leo Tolstoy. Ivan, it seems, had been counted a success all his life; he had lived so well and for so long that it came as a great shock to him when his doctor told him in the course of a routine visit that he had a serious form of cancer and did not have long to live. As Tolstoy tells the story, Ivan passes through all of the stages that we have come to recognize as the stages of death and dying. First, he denies the news: this could not be happening to *me.* Then, he is angry about it: why should this be happening to me? And, in a true-to-life moment in the story, Tolstoy describes Ivan's anger even against his wife and children whose visits to his bedside only remind him that they are healthy and he is not. After anger, Ivan tries to bargain with God, promising so much reform, so many changed habits in exchange for a longer lease on life.

The fourth stage is the most crucial of all, and it is the stage that Jesus has reached in his moment of fear at abandonment. Ivan feels as if he is being thrust into a dark bag by some "invisible, resistless force." "He struggled," says Tolstoy, "as a man condemned to death struggles in the hands of the executioner, knowing that he cannot save himself. And every moment he felt that despite all his efforts he was drawing nearer and nearer to what terrified him."

Ivan resists being thrust into the bag because he wants to justify the way he has lived up to this point. He is depressed and anxious at the thought that so much life should count for nothing. Suddenly he sees a light and knows that even now it is not too late to do something different with his life, to do what he calls "the right thing." Even if nothing has counted up to now, it is still time to act. Seeing his family around his bedside, seeing their tears, Ivan moves out to them with compassion. He is sorry for them and does not want to cause them any further hurt, and so he actively accepts his death as a final gift to them. His death will be a release from further suffering: for him and for them. Once he says, "Let the pain be; let the death be," he finds the joy of going forward—through the dark bag and into light.

The cross of Jesus is the crisis of his entire public life, and this word from the cross is the turning point of the crisis. Up to now, Jesus has emptied himself of all he can give. He has even emptied himself of the need to know why this has had to be. He comes to the point where, in all senses of the word, this is a death he freely accepts.

Once Jesus does this, he transforms once and for all the meaning of the cross. To the eyes of the world, it is foolishness; to the eyes of faith, it is wisdom. To the eyes of the world, it is weakness; to the eyes of faith, it is strength. The cross is a sign of contradiction, overturning the wisdom of every age and putting to shame any pride in human power.

Through the cross, we have reason to hope that God understands what it means to walk in the valley of the shadow of death and to suffer fear and abandonment there because Jesus really cried out, "My God, my God, why have you forsaken me?" At the same time, we believe that in Christ the final words of Psalm 22 have also come true: that the Father does not spurn or disdain the wretched person in misery, nor does God turn his face from her or him, but when that person cries out to God, God hears (v. 25).

It is through Christ, then, that we have reason to trust that not even death can defeat the faithful love of God for his people.

FIFTH WORD

"I thirst."
John 19:28-29

The thirst of Jesus is a painful result of crucifixion. And so, when we hear Jesus complain that he is thirsty, we are reminded again in human terms of how much it costs to teach us about the mystery of evil and about the faithful, forgiving love of God.

But since this word comes from the Gospel of John, we should expect that beyond the literal meaning there lies a spiritual meaning as well. John makes this especially clear by saying that "Jesus knew that everything had now been completed" and so "to fulfill the scripture perfectly, he said, 'I am thirsty.'" For John, the thirst of Jesus brings to a climax the meaning of the Jewish scriptures.

Perhaps Jesus alludes to a specific passage of those scriptures; for example, the lament of Psalm 69 in which the speaker, obviously a true and suffering Israelite, complains, "When I was thirsty, they gave me vinegar to drink." If Jesus is thinking of this psalm in particular, then he is applying to himself the hopes of Israel for a Messiah and is reminding us in the words of this psalm that God will hear his servant's cries of suffering and will rebuild the hopes of his people.

But it is more likely that the words of Jesus apply in a much broader way to the words of the Jewish scriptures and fulfill them in a much deeper sense. For example, we remember that in his agony in the garden of Gethsemane, Jesus prayed that he would not have to drink the cup that the Father would give him. The "cup" is a Jewish expression which has two meanings: the first is that of a bitter drink full of painful suffering. Prophets like Isaiah (51:17) used to speak of the cup of God's wrath that Israel would have to drink as a punishment for its sins; and the Psalmist, too, had spoken of the cup of frothing wine in God's hands, a cup heavily drugged, which all of the wicked would have to drain to the dregs. No wonder Jesus prayed to be spared from drinking this cup—if at all possible. He prayed that he would not have to be tested to the extent that he would be.

But evil is strong, and it makes victims especially of the innocent. Jesus was not spared the worst that wickedness and ignorance could do. We do not know why he had to suffer what he did. We only know that he freely accepted it, once he realized that it had to be. He learned obedience through what he suffered, and he drank the cup of wrath that he did not in any sense deserve.

Now, there is, in addition to the cup of wrath, another kind of cup in the scriptures: a cup of blessing and of thanksgiving. This is one the faithful servant of God takes up and drinks to his health. There is even the idea that even God is a kind of cup, holding the destiny of his people and giving them to drink of himself.

And so, when Jesus says, "I thirst," he fulfills the scriptures because he drinks of the cup God has to give. It is a cup of wrath and a cup of blessing all at once: it is a cup of wrath because from it the mystery of evil is drained to the dregs; it is a cup of blessing, because through what he suffers, Jesus discovers for himself, humanly speaking, and reveals to us, the never-ending and faithful love of God.

It is because he thirsts to do the will of the one who has sent him that, according to John, Jesus prayed at the last supper, "Am I not to drink the cup the Father has given me?" The more you search the scriptures, as John invites us to do, the more you discover that the thirst of Jesus is like the thirst of the people of Israel itself for God alone and for God above all things.

For example, from the time of their wandering in the desert to the time of the prophet Isaiah, the people put their trust in God and described their hope for deliverance at God's hands in the words of hunger and thirst: "God, you are my God, I am seeking you; my soul is thirsting for you, my flesh is longing for you, like a land parched, weary, and without water" (Psalm 63). Or, in the words of Psalm 143, the faithful soul who is being hounded to death and is full of fear, remembers the mercy of God and says, "I recall the days of old, I remember all that you did, I ponder your deeds; I stretch out my hands; like thirsty ground, I yearn for you."

For God's people, God is the good shepherd who leads them beside the still water and lets them drink deep; he revives their drooping spirit. He gives them water even in the desert—even from the rock—showing that he is always with them, even when they cannot see him and even when they complain bitterly that he has abandoned them to death.

God is food and water for his people; he is life itself and if they take him at his word—if they eat and drink what he offers freely—they will live. "Come to the water, all you who are thirsty," says Isaiah; "pay attention, come to me; listen, and your soul will live" (55:1).

And Jesus said, "I thirst," knowing that everything was accomplished and wanting to fulfill the scriptures perfectly.

In this word from the cross, Jesus begins to be filled with the glory of the Father just as the parched desert revives with the early rains of spring. And as he comes into his Kingdom, we see in our Lord a clear reminder for ourselves: we, too, are made for God. As the catechism puts it so simply and so well, we are made to know, love, and serve God so that we will be happy with him forever.

Anything less than God may be good, but it does not satisfy for long. And so, if you find that you are restless and unhappy, it may be that you have been trying to find your rest and your happiness only in those goods that are offered to us—at some cost—by our culture of conspicuous consumption. It is a fact of life, not just an idea of preachers, that the thirst of the human heart cannot be satisfied by anything the eye can see or the hands can grasp. As a matter of fact, we are people who hunger and thirst for the justice, the truth, the beauty, the love that is God. And only with God will we ever be satisfied.

George Herbert the poet once put it in the form of a story:

> When God at first made man,
> Having a glass of blessings standing by,
> Let us, said he, pour on him all we can
> Let the earth's riches, which dispersed lie
> Contract into a span.
> So strength first made a way;
> Then beauty flowed, then wisdom, honor, pleasure:
> When almost all was out, God made a stay

Perceiving that alone of all his treasure
Rest in the bottom lay.
For if I should (said he)
Bestow this jewel also on my creature,
He would adore my gifts instead of me,
And rest in nature, not the God of nature:
So both should losers be.
Yet let him keep the rest
But keep them with repining restlessness.
Let him be rich and weary, that at least,
If goodness lead him not, yet weariness
May toss him to my breast.

It was to fulfill the scriptures perfectly and to direct our attention to the way of our eternal rest that Jesus asked at the last supper, "Am I not to drink the cup which the Father gives me?" And he answered his own question as he hung on the cross and cried out, "I thirst."

It is accomplished.

SIXTH WORD

"It is finished."
John 19:30-37

The sixth word from the cross, like the third and fifth words, is also from the Gospel of John, and therefore we should expect that it is a word with two meanings at once. And so it is. The work of Jesus is "finished" in the sense that there is no more to do, it is complete. But also this is the "end" in the sense that this is the "goal" of all that the Word of God has wanted to say. It is finished: the hope of the scriptures for a savior has been answered to the full.

The work of Jesus, according to John, has been a work of being brought low and of being raised high, all at once. As Jesus had promised the crowds, he is lifted up, lifted up on the cross and so brought low as far as the world is concerned. But Jesus is also lifted up in glory—all in the same hour— drawing all people to himself and putting to shame the short-sighted wisdom of the world.

The seven words from the cross, put together, are making the same point about the work of Jesus. A long tradition has taken these words from all of the Gospels and arranged them in the sequence we have today in order to make clear what kind of work Jesus does for our salvation.

As we saw in the first three words, it is a work of self-giving shown in forgiveness for the world that has judged Jesus to be an outlaw and in forgiveness for the outlaw next to him, who recognizes in the character of Christ not a criminal but a king, and who wants a share in the Kingdom. The work of Jesus is also one of care for the church and for humanity, giving them into the charge of one another so that after Jesus' death each will have a home through his Spirit.

Thanks to the work of Jesus as it is summed up on the cross, we have an especially clear manifestation of two things: God's faithful love for us and our inalienable human worth. In the words of Pope John Paul II, "In Christ and through Christ, God has revealed himself to us and has definitively drawn close to us. At the same time, in Christ and through Christ, we have acquired full awareness of our dignity, of the heights to which we are raised, of the surpassing worth of our own humanity and of the meaning of our existence."

In the fourth word, we witness the work of Jesus at a turning point. Humanly speaking, he can do no more; he has exhausted himself in complete self-giving. He feels abandoned and in desperate straits like the man in Psalm 69 who cried out, "I have stepped into deep water, and the waves are washing over me; O Lord, rescue me from the mire before I sink in. . . . Do not let the waves wash over me, nor the deep swallow me up, nor the pit close its mouth over me." At this point, the man can either give in to the pull of the mud and the rush of the waters, or he can reach up in trust and wait for the Lord to prove that he is faithful. The man, in fact, comes to trust that he can rely on the Lord, and so he prays that God will raise him up by his saving power, and he affirms his faith that God listens to the poor; God does not scorn his own people.

When Jesus chooses the way of trust, he reveals the resurrection. He shows that God is faithful indeed and reverses once and for all the judgment of the world against him. Then, in the fifth word, Jesus begins a movement toward the Father that will fill him with glory. His thirst is for the cup the Father gives him to drink, and when he drinks the cup of wrath he swallows up sin and death. At the same moment the cup of wrath becomes a cup of blessing, because Jesus proves that he is the victor, the one who conquers sin and death. He is the way, the truth, the life.

No wonder, then, that Jesus can say that his work is finished, that it has reached its goal. Jesus has transformed the meaning of the cross for all time. It is no longer merely an instrument of execution proving that the state must always have the final word. No, the cross is a sign of contradiction, overturning the verdict of the state and proving the world wrong about who has sinned and about what justice is. The cross cancels out the power of darkness by proving that the light shines on in the darkness and the darkness cannot overcome it. And so the cross not only manifests God's care for us despite the mystery of evil and human sin; the cross is, at the same time, a proclamation against all short-sighted and even cynical definitions of the good life that pass for worldly wisdom in every age.

Our pride in power *over* others is contradicted by the Lord's self-giving power *for* others. Our pride in sensual comforts of all kinds is contradicted by the thirst of Jesus for the justice and the holiness of God above all things. Our pride in riches is contradicted by his poverty. Naked we came into this world, and naked we will go out of it. Wealth certainly has its purposes, but none of them can conceal our fundamental poverty and need for the good which is God. Our use of freedom for the purpose of self-indulgence is contradicted by the nails in the feet and hands that keep Jesus riveted to the cross and tell us—if we will only hear it—that the proper use of freedom is charity.

The work of Jesus, then, is finished. And, as John goes on to tell us, the work is life-giving as well. In John's Gospel, the death of Jesus occurs after this word, and it is described in a highly significant way. Jesus, says John, bowed his head and handed over his spirit. Again, we have two senses of the word: On the one hand Jesus gives out his last breath; on the other hand, he hands over the Holy Spirit to those who would live after him in the world. He pours out his Spirit on the woman and the beloved disciple who stand at the foot of the cross. Then, from the pierced side of Jesus flow water and blood, signs of the waters of baptism and the blood of the eucharist. Together with the Holy Spirit, they are poured out on the church so that the church will have the strength and the wisdom to follow Christ to fullness of life.

This is where we come into the picture as people brought to life by the cross and bound to be witnesses of the cross in the world. If we have heard the words of Jesus with faith, then we become disciples. We commit ourselves to having that mind in us that was also in Christ Jesus. We learn what it means in our time to do the work that will let God's will be done on earth as it is in heaven.

There is a promise for those who stand by the cross and who hear the words of Christ and who become witnesses of them. The promise of Jesus is this: "If you make my words your home, you will indeed by my disciples; you will know the truth, and the truth shall make you free." In the deepest sense of this sixth word from the cross, the work of Jesus is finished only when it brings each of us and all the world to fullness of life.

SEVENTH WORD

"Father, into your hands I commit my spirit."

Luke 23:44-56

The final words from the cross come from the Gospel of Luke, and they sum up Luke's portrait of Jesus as the witness—the martyr—for the Kingdom of God. From what he says, we are to learn much not only about the relationship of Jesus to his Father, but also about how we are to imitate the Lord's example.

The words of Jesus are a prayer, taken from Psalm 31, the everyday prayer of the Jewish people. This prayerfulness of Jesus is something that Luke has wanted to emphasize throughout his entire account of the Lord's life. Only Luke, for example, mentions that Jesus was at prayer after his baptism when the Holy Spirit descended upon him. Only Luke records that when Jesus went up the mountain where he was to appear in glory before his disciples, that he went there to pray; Matthew and Mark simply mention that Jesus went up to be alone. And only Luke provides the situation in which Jesus taught us the Lord's prayer. In Matthew's Gospel, Jesus simply includes it in the sermon on the mount; it sounds almost like part of a list of instructions. But Luke tells us this: "Now it happened that Jesus was in a certain place praying, and when he had finished one of his disciples said, 'Lord, teach us to pray, as John the Baptist taught his disciples.' And Jesus said to them, 'When you pray, this is what you are to say: "Father, may your name be held holy."'" In other words, the Lord's prayer is something the disciples caught from the example of Jesus. They saw him at prayer and they saw him in action, and they wanted to know his secret. "Lord," they asked, "teach us to pray." And in his great mercy, Jesus freely taught the disciples about what he said to the Father when he was alone.

Vocal prayer, it has been said, is the soul in paraphrase; vocal prayer is the silent longing of the soul put into words. And as his last word from the cross, Jesus cries out a prayer in a loud voice, a prayer of complete trust. The prayer belongs to the people of Israel since it is taken from their book of psalms. And so, right to the end, Jesus shows himself to be one with his people, expressing his trust in his Father in terms that everyone could easily understand.

With these words, Jesus takes his death into his own hands and, after freely accepting it, makes it his project, that is, death becomes the way he throws himself forward. That is what a project is: something cast in front of you. Jesus uses his death to throw himself forward from this world to the Father, from the hands of sinful humanity into the hands of God. "Father, into your hands I commit my spirit." And with this forward movement, Jesus makes the sacrifice of himself complete.

We need to realize a little more exactly what Jesus is doing. When we think of sacrifice we usually think only of something difficult; necessary, perhaps, but difficult all the same. We forget the word "sacrifice" means to "make holy" by giving it over to God. In the Jewish law, this was done by taking something like an animal which takes the place of oneself and then killing it in order to remove it completely from ordinary use. This was one way of showing that you yourself were trying to give yourself over to God, too. It might take time, but your life was a sacrifice all the same. It was an attempt to become like God—to become holy—in order to find the fullness of life which is God.

Well, on the cross, the sacrifice of Jesus is complete. He projects himself into the hands of his Father and comes home. Of course, the death and the homecoming of Jesus are not events that happen only to himself. No, he is the head of his body, the church. Where he has gone, we are bound to follow, that is, if we catch something from his example and live out our lives in his spirit.

According to Luke, this is precisely what begins to happen on Calvary. Even as Jesus breathes his last, the people catch something of what this death is telling them. For example, the Roman centurion, a gentile, praises God and says, "Truly, this was an upright man." He sees already that Jesus is innocent and so he comes half way to faith by at least rejecting the Roman version of history. The centurion sees the cross as a contradiction of what his superior officers and Pontius Pilate would like to have him believe. The judgment of the world is brought under judgment itself in the centurion's word, "This was an upright man."

And then, says Luke, "when the crowds who had gathered for the spectacle saw what had happened, they went home beating their breasts." In other words, the witness of Jesus to the Kingdom of God is beginning to bear fruit through repentance of sin.

It is in the Acts of the Apostles, also written by Luke,

that we see the full force of the Spirit of Jesus catching fire in the lives of the disciples who are the people of God, the church. As St. Stephen is brought out to suffer a martyr's death, he too, like his master, forgives his enemies and, borrowing as well the words of Psalm 31, prays, "Lord Jesus, receive my spirit." As if by chance, Saul of Tarsus is there and consents to the death. He holds the clothes of the executioners while they do their work. And the message becomes clear: the witness of Jesus is being caught up by disciples like Stephen and then carried forward by people like Saul who, along with changing his mind and his life, changes his name to Paul and then brings the gospel from Jerusalem and Judea northward into Samaria and even to the ends of the earth.

We who have "heard" the seven words from the cross and reflected on them are only the latest in a long line of listeners. It is up to us, now, in our time, to hear in these words the summing up of the mind of Christ. We are to let these words sink into our hearts where our deepest questions lie waiting for an answer, questions like: Do I matter? Will I be safe? Am I forgiven? Am I understood? What should I do with my freedom? Let these words from the cross be our answer and an anchor of hope for us.

When Jesus dies, he does so as head of his body the church. He goes before us, showing us the way. He is like the anchor of a boat thrown ahead into the deep and taking sure hold at a place we cannot see. But thanks to that anchor, we know that the mystery in which we live and move has a bottom to it; and we have reason to believe that at the bottom of it all is the unfathomable mercy and wisdom of God. "Praise the Lord, all you nations; praise him, all you peoples. For the mercy of the Lord has been confirmed upon us; and the fidelity of the Lord endures forever."